THE SECRETS OF DEVELOPING YOUR INNER STRENGTH

A GUIDE TO PERSONAL GROWTH AND DEVELOPMENT

DR. JAGADEESH PILLAI

|| Dedicate to all wisdom seekers around the world ||

Contents

Contents

Prayer

**"Om Poornamadah Poornamidam Poornat
Poornamudachyate,Poornasya Poornamaadaya
Poornamevavavashishyate,Om Shantih, Shantih, Shantih"**

*The literal interpretation of this mantra is: That which is
Absolute, This which is Absolute, Absolute arises from Absolute,
If Absolute is removed from Absolute, Absolute remains
OM Peace, Peace, Peace.*

ᗡᗡᗡ

About The Author

Dr. Jagadeesh Pillai is a renowned Guinness World Record holder, writer, and researcher hailing from Varanasi, also known as the abode of Lord Shiva. With a Ph.D. in Vedic Science and a range of creative ideas and achievements, he is a true polymath. He is the author of more than 100 books including Research Publications. Although his roots can be traced back to Kerala, the people of Varanasi hold him in high regard and affectionately consider him one of their own.

Dr. Pillai has achieved four Guinness World Records in the following subjects:

"Script to Screen" - In this record, Dr. Pillai produced and directed an animation film within the shortest time possible, breaking the previous record set by Canadians. He has also received numerous national and international awards and recognitions for this achievement.

Longest Line of Postcards - For this record, Dr. Pillai created a line of 16,300 postcards on the occasion of the 163rd anniversary of Indian Postal Day. The event also included a questionnaire about the Indian flag.

Largest Poster Awareness Campaign - Dr. Pillai designed an awareness campaign on the subject of "Beti Bachao - Beti Padhao" (Save the Girl Child - Educate the Girl Child) to achieve this record.

Largest Envelope - In tribute to the Indian Prime Minister's

"Make in India" initiative, Dr. Pillai created a 4000 square meter envelope using waste paper to achieve this record.

Attempted - **70000 Candles on a 210 kg Cake** - To celebrate the 70th Indian Independence Day, Dr. Pillai attempted to light 70,000 candles on a 210 kg cake, which was recorded in World Records India.

Attempted - **Documentary on Dhamek Stupa of Sarnath in 17 Languages** - Dr. Pillai attempted to create a documentary on the Dhamek Stupa of Sarnath, dubbing it in 17 different languages. The result of this attempt is currently awaiting confirmation from the Guinness World Records.

Dr. Pillai is skilled in teaching the Bhagavad Gita, a Hindu scripture, and is popular among young people. He has helped many young people improve their lives through his motivational teachings.

In addition to teaching, he has composed and sung numerous Sanskrit Bhajans and patriotic songs.

He has also written and directed several short films and documentaries for awareness campaigns, and has volunteered with the police in both UP and Kerala to spread awareness about various issues through videos and photography.

Incredibly, he has produced and directed over 100 documentaries about the city of Varanasi, all on his own.

He has also helped and guided more than 25 boys and girls to achieve world records through creative and innovative methods. He is a multifaceted person who uses his intellect and the blessings given to him by God to excel in various areas. He is both a teacher and a student, always learning and teaching, and is able to master any subject he comes across.

He is a selfless social activist and motivational speaker who has overcome struggles and failures to become a successful and enthusiastic individual with a rich life experience.

In addition to his work with the Bhagavad Gita, he is also an efficient Tarot card reader, Astro-Vastu consultant, and a talented singer and composer. He has sung the entire Ram Charita Manas and Bhagavad Gita in his own compositions, and has sung the phrase "Lokah Samastha Sukhino Bhavantu" in 50 different languages. He is currently working on a detailed and scientific study of Vedas, Upanishads, Puranas, and the Bhagavad Gita. He has also composed and sung the Hanuman Chalisa and Gayatri Mantra in 108 and 1008 different compositions, respectively.

Awards - Four Times Guinness World Records, Winner of Mahatma Gandhi Vishwa Shanti Puraskar, Mahatma Gandhi Global Peace Ambassador, Kashi Ratna Award, Dr. APJ Abdul Kalam Motivational Person of the Year 2017, Mother Teresa Award, Indira Gandhi Priyadarshini Award, Bharat Vikas Ratna Award, Udyog Ratna Award, Vigyan Prasar Award, Poorvanchal Ratn Samman.

ॐॐॐ

Preface

This book, "Secret of Developing Your Inner Strength: A Guide to Personal Growth and Development," is a comprehensive guide that will help readers to develop their inner strength and achieve personal growth and development. Inner strength is a vital component of leading a fulfilling life and achieving success, and this book provides readers with the tools and strategies they need to develop it.

The book is divided into 11 chapters, each of which is designed to help readers understand and develop a specific aspect of inner strength. The chapters cover topics such as mindfulness, self-awareness, emotional intelligence, resilience, positive thinking, time management, communication skills, and stress management.

Throughout the book, readers will find practical exercises, techniques, and strategies that they can use to develop their inner strength. These are based on the latest research and are designed to be easy to understand and apply.

I believe that anyone can develop their inner strength, and this book is intended to provide readers with the knowledge and tools they need to do so. Whether you are looking to improve your relationships, achieve your goals, or simply lead a more fulfilling life, this book will provide you with the guidance you need to get there.

My goal in writing this book is to empower readers to take control of their lives and achieve their full potential. I hope that it will inspire and motivate you to begin your own journey of personal growth and development.

ᖘᖘᖘ

ONE

Introduction: Understanding the Importance of Inner Strength

Inner strength is the ability to handle difficult situations and emotions with grace, resilience, and courage. It is the foundation of mental and emotional well-being and is essential for achieving success in all areas of life. People with strong inner strength are able to navigate through life's challenges with ease and emerge victorious. They possess the ability to stay calm and composed under pressure, to think clearly and make sound decisions, to maintain positive relationships, and to achieve their goals.

Inner strength is not something that one is born with, but

rather something that can be developed over time. It is a combination of mental, emotional, and physical strength that can be strengthened through practice and perseverance. The key to developing inner strength is to understand that it is not about being perfect, but about being able to handle difficult situations and emotions in a way that promotes growth and development.

Readers must learn about the importance of inner strength and how it can enhance their personal growth and development. It will also provide an overview of the various aspects of inner strength, including emotional intelligence, resilience, positive thinking, and time management, among others. Additionally, readers will be introduced to the concept of mindfulness and how it can be used to promote inner strength.

"Introduction: Understanding the Importance of Inner Strength" is an essential chapter for readers who want to develop their inner strength and achieve personal growth and development. It provides a comprehensive understanding of what inner strength is and why it is important, and lays the foundation for the rest of the book. By reading this chapter, readers will be equipped with the knowledge and tools necessary to embark on their journey towards inner strength and a fulfilling life.

ᗡᗡᗡ

"The only limit to our realization of tomorrow will be our doubts of today."

❦❦❦

TWO

IDENTIFYING YOUR WEAKNESSES: A SELF-ASSESSMENT

Self-assessment is an important step in the journey towards inner strength. By identifying your personal weaknesses, you can begin to work on them and make them strengths. This process requires honesty and self-reflection, and it is important to be kind and compassionate towards yourself during this process.

One effective way to identify your weaknesses is to ask yourself questions such as "What are my emotional triggers?" "What are the areas in my life where I struggle the most?" "What are the habits or patterns that hold me back?" "What are the things that I avoid doing because I find them difficult or uncomfortable?"

Another approach is to ask others for feedback. You can ask your friends, family, or colleagues for their honest opinion about your strengths and weaknesses. This can be valuable as it can provide you with a different perspective and help you identify areas that you may not have noticed yourself.

Once you have identified your weaknesses, it is important to prioritize which ones to work on first. It's best to start with the areas that have the most impact on your life and that can be improved relatively quickly. It's important to remember that developing inner strength is a long-term process, and it's important to be patient with yourself.

"Identifying Your Weaknesses: A Self-Assessment" is a critical chapter that helps readers to take the first step in developing their inner strength by identifying areas that need improvement. By being honest with themselves and seeking feedback from others, readers can gain a better understanding of their strengths and weaknesses and set a clear path towards personal growth and development.

ϷϷϷ

THREE

SETTING GOALS AND PRIORITIZING: ACHIEVING SUCCESS

Setting clear and specific goals is essential for achieving success and developing inner strength. Without goals, it can be difficult to focus and stay motivated, and it is easy to get sidetracked by distractions. Setting goals provides a sense of direction and purpose, and helps to keep you on track towards achieving your desired outcome.

When setting goals, it is important to be realistic and to set both short-term and long-term goals. This will help to create a sense of progression and momentum, and will also make it easier to measure your progress. Additionally, it is important to break down larger goals into smaller, more manageable tasks.

Once the goals are set, it is important to prioritize them. Not all goals are created equal, and it is essential to focus on the most important ones first. This means identifying the goals that will have the most impact on your life and that align with your personal growth and development. Prioritizing your goals will help you to stay focused and to avoid wasting time and energy on less important tasks.

"Setting Goals and Prioritizing: Achieving Success" is an important chapter that helps readers to set and achieve their goals and stay focused on their personal growth and development. By setting clear and specific goals, prioritizing them, and breaking them down into smaller tasks, readers can increase their chances of success and develop their inner strength.

ᏇᏇᏇ

"You are never too old to set another goal or
to dream a new dream."

ᗞᗞᗞ

FOUR

MINDFULNESS AND SELF-AWARENESS: THE POWER OF PRESENCE

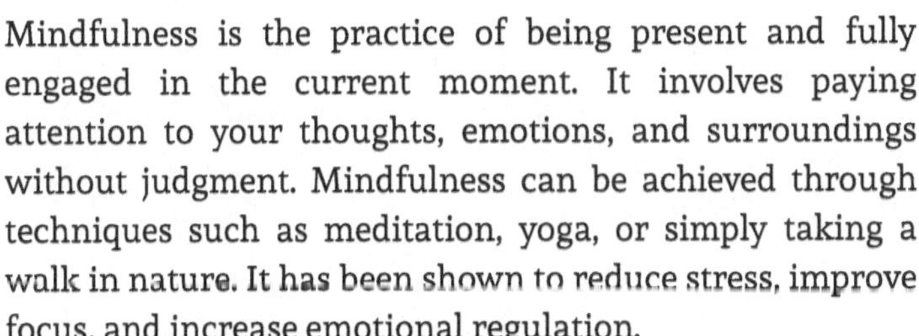

Mindfulness is the practice of being present and fully engaged in the current moment. It involves paying attention to your thoughts, emotions, and surroundings without judgment. Mindfulness can be achieved through techniques such as meditation, yoga, or simply taking a walk in nature. It has been shown to reduce stress, improve focus, and increase emotional regulation.

Self-awareness, on the other hand, is the ability to understand your own thoughts, emotions, and behaviors. It involves being aware of your own strengths and weaknesses, as well as how your actions and reactions affect others. By increasing self-awareness, you can gain a better understanding of your own thoughts and emotions and how they affect your behavior.

The combination of mindfulness and self-awareness can be a powerful tool for developing inner strength. By being present in the moment, you can gain a better understanding of your thoughts and emotions, allowing you to make better decisions and respond more effectively to difficult situations. Additionally, by being self-aware, you can identify patterns of behavior that may be holding you back and work to change them.

"Mindfulness and Self-Awareness: The Power of Presence" is an important chapter that helps readers to understand the importance of being present and self-aware in the journey towards developing inner strength. By practicing mindfulness and increasing self-awareness, readers can gain a better understanding of their thoughts, emotions, and behaviors, and make positive changes that lead to personal growth and development.

ppp

"The only way to do great work is to love
what you do."

♡♡♡

FIVE

EMOTIONAL INTELLIGENCE: MANAGING YOUR EMOTIONS

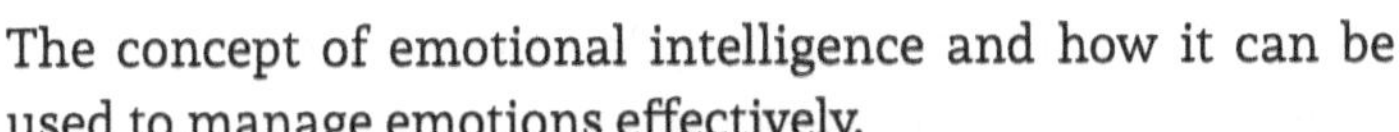

The concept of emotional intelligence and how it can be used to manage emotions effectively.

Emotional intelligence (EI) refers to the ability to recognize, understand, and manage one's own emotions and the emotions of others. It includes skills such as self-awareness, self-regulation, motivation, empathy, and social skills. People with high emotional intelligence are better equipped to handle difficult situations, build strong relationships, and achieve their goals.

Managing emotions effectively is a key aspect of emotional intelligence. This means being able to recognize, understand, and express your emotions in a healthy and appropriate way. It also involves being able to regulate your emotions, so that they don't overpower you and interfere with your ability to think clearly and make sound decisions.

One way to improve emotional intelligence is to practice mindfulness and self-awareness. By being present in the moment and understanding your own thoughts and emotions, you can gain a better understanding of what triggers certain emotions and how to respond to them in a healthy way. Additionally, learning techniques such as cognitive-behavioral therapy, deep breathing, and self-reflection can help to improve emotional regulation.

"Emotional Intelligence: Managing Your Emotions" is an important chapter that helps readers to understand the importance of emotional intelligence and how it can be used to manage emotions effectively. By developing emotional intelligence, readers can improve their ability to recognize, understand, and regulate their emotions, leading to personal growth and development.

ϷϷϷ

"The greatest glory in living lies not in never falling, but in rising every time we fall."

♡♡♡

SIX

BUILDING RESILIENCE: OVERCOMING OBSTACLES

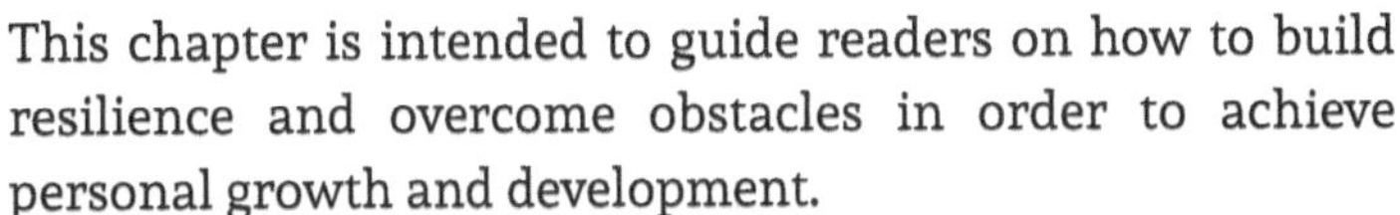

This chapter is intended to guide readers on how to build resilience and overcome obstacles in order to achieve personal growth and development.

Resilience is the ability to bounce back from adversity and to adapt to change. It is a key component of inner strength and is essential for achieving success in all areas of life. People who are resilient are better equipped to handle difficult situations and to overcome obstacles.

Building resilience involves developing a growth mindset, learning from failures, and developing a support system. A growth mindset is the belief that you can develop your abilities and overcome challenges through effort and practice. By learning from failures, you can gain a better understanding of what went wrong and how to do better next time. A support system is a group of people who you can rely on for emotional and practical support, such as friends, family, or a therapist.

Other strategies to build resilience include practicing mindfulness, engaging in physical activity, and maintaining a healthy lifestyle. Mindfulness can help you to stay present in the moment and to manage stress. Physical activity can help to improve mood and reduce stress. Eating a healthy diet and getting enough sleep can also help to reduce stress and improve overall well-being.

"Building Resilience: Overcoming Obstacles" is an important chapter that helps readers to understand the importance of resilience and how it can be developed. By learning about the strategies for building resilience, readers can develop the ability to bounce back from adversity and overcome obstacles, leading to personal growth and development.

ppp

"You miss 100% of the shots you don't take."

♡♡♡

SEVEN

POSITIVE THINKING AND ATTITUDE: THE POWER OF PERSPECTIVE

How to develop a positive mindset and attitude to achieve personal growth and development.

Positive thinking and attitude can have a powerful impact on your mental and emotional well-being. It is the ability to focus on the good things in life, to find the positive in negative situations, and to maintain a hopeful outlook. People with a positive mindset tend to be more resilient, optimistic, and successful in achieving their goals.

Developing a positive attitude involves changing the way

you think about yourself and the world around you. One way to do this is to practice gratitude, which is the practice of being thankful for what you have in your life. This can help to shift your focus from what you lack to what you have. Another way to develop a positive attitude is to practice positive affirmations, which are positive statements that you repeat to yourself to change your mindset.

It's also important to practice self-compassion, which is the ability to be kind and understanding towards yourself when things go wrong. Self-compassion helps to reduce self-criticism and negative self-talk and can improve your ability to cope with difficult situations.

Another key aspect of positive thinking and attitude is perspective. By shifting your perspective, you can change the way you see a situation and find a more positive solution. This can involve looking at a problem from different angles or considering the bigger picture.

"Positive Thinking and Attitude: The Power of Perspective" is an important chapter that helps readers to understand the importance of positive thinking and attitude and how it can be developed. By learning about the strategies for developing a positive mindset and attitude, readers can improve their mental and emotional well-being and achieve personal growth and development.

ppp

"Success is not final, failure is not fatal: it is
the courage to continue that counts."

ᐯᐯᐯ

EIGHT

TIME MANAGEMENT AND PRIORITIZATION: MAKING THE MOST OF YOUR TIME

How to effectively manage their time and prioritize their tasks in order to achieve personal growth and development.

Effective time management is essential for achieving success and developing inner strength. It involves setting clear goals, making a plan of action, and staying organized. By managing your time effectively, you can ensure that you are spending your time on the things that are most important and that align with your personal growth and development.

One way to improve time management is to prioritize tasks. This means identifying the most important tasks and focusing on them first. It's also important to set deadlines for yourself and to break down larger tasks into smaller, more manageable ones.

Another key aspect of time management is to eliminate distractions and to stay focused. This may involve turning off your phone, closing unnecessary tabs on your computer, or finding a quiet space to work.

In addition to managing time, it's important to take regular breaks to re-energize and refresh the mind. This could involve taking a short walk, meditating, or doing some stretching exercises.

"Time Management and Prioritization: Making the Most of Your Time" is an important chapter that helps readers to understand the importance of effective time management and how it can be developed. By learning about the strategies for managing time and prioritizing tasks, readers can improve their ability to focus on what's important and achieve personal growth and development.

ЬЬЬ

"The best way to predict your future is to
create it."

ᗡᗡᗡ

NINE

COMMUNICATION SKILLS: BUILDING STRONG RELATIONSHIPS

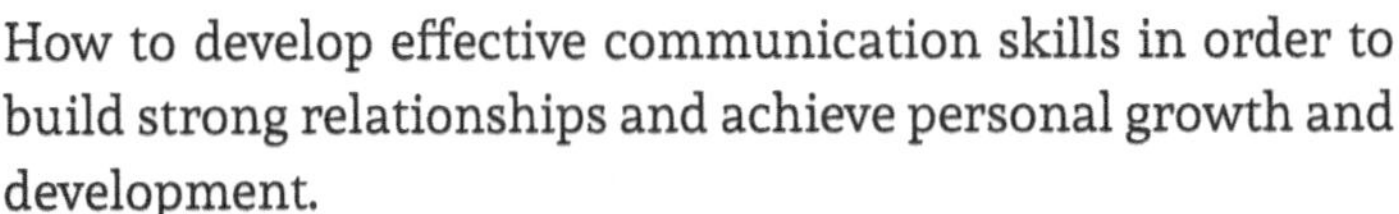

How to develop effective communication skills in order to build strong relationships and achieve personal growth and development.

Effective communication is a key component of building strong relationships. It involves the ability to clearly express your thoughts and feelings, to actively listen, and to understand the perspectives of others. By developing your communication skills, you can improve your ability to connect with others, to resolve conflicts, and to achieve your goals.

One way to improve communication skills is to practice active listening. This involves giving your full attention to the person you are talking to, and making an effort to understand their perspective. Additionally, it's important to use "I" statements when expressing yourself, which can help to avoid blame and defensiveness.

Another way to improve communication skills is to learn the art of compromise. This means finding a middle ground that satisfies both parties in a dispute. It's also important to practice empathy, which is the ability to understand and share the feelings of others.

Finally, it's important to be aware of nonverbal communication such as body language, tone of voice, and facial expressions. These can convey just as much information as the words you use and can be the key to effective communication.

"Communication Skills: Building Strong Relationships" is an important chapter that helps readers to understand the importance of effective communication skills and how it can be developed. By learning about the strategies for improving communication skills, readers can build stronger relationships, improve their ability to connect with others, and achieve personal growth and development.

ᐅᐅᐅ

"The only true wisdom is in knowing you know nothing."

❤❤❤

TEN

STRESS MANAGEMENT: COPING WITH LIFE'S CHALLENGES

How to effectively manage stress in order to cope with life's challenges and achieve personal growth and development.

Stress is a natural response to challenging situations, but when it becomes chronic, it can have a negative impact on your mental and physical health. Effective stress management is essential for achieving success and developing inner strength.

One way to manage stress is to identify the sources of stress in your life. This can involve keeping a stress journal, where you write down the events or situations that cause stress, as well as your physical and emotional reactions to them. Once you have identified the sources of stress, you can develop a plan to address them.

Another effective stress management technique is to practice relaxation techniques such as deep breathing, meditation, yoga, or progressive muscle relaxation. These techniques can help to calm the mind and body and reduce feelings of stress.

It's also important to maintain a healthy lifestyle, which includes getting enough sleep, eating a balanced diet, and exercising regularly. These activities can help to reduce stress, improve mood, and promote overall well-being.

In addition, it's essential to practice self-care, which can be defined as the practices that are necessary to maintain and improve one's physical, mental and emotional health. This can include activities such as reading, spending time in nature, listening to music or having a hobby.

ppp

"The secret of getting ahead is getting
started."

❥❥❥

ELEVEN

CONCLUSION: HARNESSING YOUR INNER STRENGTH FOR A FULFILLING LIFE.

Throughout the book, readers have learned about the importance of inner strength and the various techniques and strategies for developing it. They have been introduced to concepts such as mindfulness, self-awareness, emotional intelligence, resilience, positive thinking, time management, communication skills, and stress management.

To harness your inner strength, it is important to take a holistic approach and to focus on multiple areas of your life. This includes taking care of your physical, mental, and emotional well-being, setting clear goals, and making a plan of action. It also involves being mindful of your thoughts and emotions, developing self-awareness, building resilience, and developing strong relationships.

In conclusion, inner strength is a vital component of personal growth and development. By developing inner strength, readers can achieve success, build strong relationships, and lead a fulfilling life. The book has provided readers with a roadmap for continued personal growth and development, and readers are encouraged to continue to practice and apply the strategies outlined in the book in order to achieve their goals and live a fulfilling life.

ÞÞÞ

*"Believe in yourself and all that you are.
Know that there is something inside you that
is greater than any obstacle."*

♡♡♡

Other Books Of The Author

1. The Moments When I Met God
2. Kashiyile Theertha Pathangal
3. GURU GYAN VANI
4. Abhiprerak Gita
5. ASSI SE JAIN GHAT TAK
6. Hopelessness of Arjuna
7. The Soul and It's True Nature
8. Sense of Action (Karma)
9. Action through Wisdom
10. Action through Wisdom
11. THEORY AND PRACTICAL OF EVERY ACTION
12. LOGICAL UNDERSTANDING OF THE SUPREME
13. THE IMPERISHABLE SUPREME
14. Yatra Nishadraj se Hanuman Ghat Tak
15. Yatra Karnatak Ghat se Raja Ghat Tak
16. Yatra Pandey Ghat se Prayagraj Ghat Tak
17. Yatra Ranjendra Prasad Ghat se Dattatreya Ghat Tak
18. YaatraSindhiya Ghat se Gwaliar Ghat Tak
19. Yatra Mangala Gauri Ghat se Hanuman Gadhi Ghat Tak
20. Yatra Gaay Ghat Se Nishad Ghat Tak
21. MAA GANGA, GHATEN EVM UTSAV
22. Ganga Arti Dev Deepavali evam Any Utsav
23. Potentials of Digitalized India
24. VEDIC CONSCIOUSNESS
25. A Brief Introduction to Vedic Science
26. Kashi ke Barah Jyotirling
27. IMPACT OF MOTIVATION
28. Let's have a Milky Way Journey
29. Color Therapy in a Nutshell

59. The Holistic Cow: A Look at the Physical, Spiritual, and Cultural Importance of Cows in India
60. Arts of Healing
61. Exploring the Divine
62. Understanding Five Elements
63. The Etymology of Ram
64. Symbols of India
65. Voice of Change (About Speeches of Great Men)
66. She Speaks (About Speeches of Great Women)
67. Patriotism on Celluloid – Brief About Patriotic Films
68. The Music of Motivation: A Brief Guide to Inspirational Film Songs
69. Unlocking the Secrets of the Dashopanishads
70. A Cultural Mosaic
71. Ancient Traditions, Modern Minds
72. Ecos of Ancient Wisdom
73. Beneath the Surface
74. From Temples to Ashrams
75. Sages of the Subcontinent
76. The Art of Healling (Ayurveda, Yoga & Naturopathy)
77. Indian Kitchen
78. The Festivals of India
79. The Indian Epics Retold
80. The Power of Mantras
81. The Indian River Ganges
82. The Indian Architecture
83. Rites of Passage
84. The Indian Silk Road
85. The Indian Literature
86. The Indian Villages
87. The Indian Folks & Crafts
88. The Way of Buddha
89. The Ramayan of Tulsidas

❧❧❧

Contact

DR. JAGADEESH PILLAI

PhD in Vedic Science

Four Times Guinness World Record Holder

Winner of Mahatma Gandhi Vishwa Shanti Puraskar and
Global Peace Ambassador

Gemology, Astro & Vastu Consultant - Spiritual Counselor

Consultant for designing World Record Ideas

Efficient Tarot Card Reader

9839093003

myrichindia@gmail.com

drjagadeeshpillai@facebook

drjagadeeshpillai@instagram

jagadeeshpillai@youtube

www. JAGADEESHPILLAI.com

ϷϷϷ

|| LOKAHA SAMASTHAHA SUKHINO BHAVANTU ||

• 51 •

9 798889 512523